Animals from Head to Tail

TURTLES FROM HEAD TO TAIL

By Jen Trifer

Please visit our website, www.garethstevens.com. For a free color catalog of all our high-quality books, call toll free 1-800-542-2595 or fax 1-877-542-2596.

Cataloging-in-Publication Data

Names: Trifer, Jen.
Title: Turtles from head to tail / Jen Trifer.
Description: New York : Gareth Stevens Publishing, 2017. | Series: Animals from head to tail | Includes index.
Identifiers: ISBN 9781482449570 (pbk.) | ISBN 9781482445404 (library bound) | ISBN 9781482445282 (6 pack)
Subjects: LCSH: Turtles–Juvenile literature.
Classification: LCC QL666.C5 T75 2017 | DDC 597.92–dc23

First Edition

Published in 2017 by
Gareth Stevens Publishing
111 East 14th Street, Suite 349
New York, NY 10003

Editor: Ryan Nagelhout
Designer: Katelyn E. Reynolds

Photo credits: Cover, p. 1 Joseph M. Arseneau/Shutterstock.com; p. 5 Marc Parsons/Shutterstock.com; p. 7 Ryan M. Bolton/Shutterstock.com; p. 9 poo/Shutterstock.com; pp. 11, 24 (neck) Cloudia Spinner/Shutterstock.com; pp. 13, 24 (carapace) Mr. SUTTIPON YAKHAM/Shutterstock.com; p. 15 bireleycrayon/Shutterstock.com; p. 17 Saranya Loisamut/Shutterstock.com; p. 19 Matt9122/Shutterstock.com; p. 21 nokty/Shutterstock.com; p. 23 Iryna Loginova/Shutterstock.com.

Printed in the United States of America

CPSIA compliance information: Batch #CS16GS: For further information contact Gareth Stevens, New York, New York at 1-800-542-2595.

Contents

Turtles have hard mouths.
This is called a beak.

Many have a strong bite!

They don't have ears.

Some have long necks.

Turtles have a hard shell.
This is called a carapace.

Their shell
keeps them safe.

They are slow on land.

Some turtles live
in the sea.

Sea turtle legs
are like fins.
This helps them swim.

Turtles have tails, too!

Words to Know

carapace

neck

Index